W9-ABX-152

OLDER AND WISER

To Gunilla,
my beloved life partner

OLDER
AND
WISER

INSPIRATION AND ADVICE
FOR RETIRING BABY BOOMERS

DAG SEBASTIAN AHLANDER
TRANSLATED BY CORY KLINGSPORN

SKYHORSE PUBLISHING

*All quotes are translated from the
Swedish as they appear in
the original edition.*

Library of Congress Cataloging-in-Publication
Data is available on file.
Print ISBN: 978-1-62914-417-7
Ebook ISBN: 978-1-63220-073-0
Printed in China

TOWARD GREAT PERSPECTIVES

WE BABY BOOMERS have practically added an entire life onto our lifespans. Swedish men now live an average of eighty years (and Americans aren't far behind), and more men than ever before live to both eighty-five and ninety—without being in constant pain, as used to be the norm. Our generation has had opportunities that few before us ever did; indeed, it almost feels like we made the dream of eternal life a reality. We grew up during the Golden Age of the Market Economy, and now we can enjoy the warming glow of the setting sun.

Our generation is so big that it has, thus far, left its mark on everything that has come its way. In Sweden we are referred to as the '40s kids, in America as the Baby Boomers. Through our size alone, we're creating a new age group, the "young elderly," just as we once created the teenager and youth counterculture. Nah, real old age can wait! One obvious fact is that society as a whole is aging because we are aging—that's how many of us there are. Another is that we older folk seem to be necessary for maintaining activity in many spheres of society.

Local politics couldn't do without us. We've become an ever-heavier part of the electorate, and thus shifted politics in our own direction. No retirees are forced to give up on politics. We're the ones sitting at the helm of boards of local organizations, doing much of the voluntary work. We comprise a disproportionately large portion of small-business owners outside of the big cities. Activity in rural areas would absolutely not survive without us.

There is, quite simply, a silent revolution going on. We older folk are also putting more of our money to use in different ways: travel, experiences, culture, health and social care, and thereby affecting the overall alignment of consumption, both private and public.

THE POLITICIANS TELL us that we must work longer, indeed, perhaps all the way until we're seventy-five, because otherwise, our retirement money will run out. Professionals and managers who are on top are more and more willing to stay on the job as long as they can. But most of us don't want to work that long, not at the same old jobs, and certainly not full-time, at any rate. We want to be active on our own terms, doing the things that interest us. This is how we can do some good while living a good life.

Besides, society needs stability and experience now more than ever. It can't tolerate any more risky young investors and economic crashes.

The Roman philosopher and statesman Cicero wrote: "Old age will only be respected if it fights for itself, maintains its rights, avoids dependence on anyone, and asserts control over its own to the last breath."

Old age is not an interest group. It is universally human. Only if we are lucky will we be old.

MANY OF US can imagine assignments and volunteer projects—but on our terms, and certainly not full time. Becoming King of the Hill doesn't matter anymore. Jealousy can finally subside. Life is not a zero-sum game. Most of us want to devote ourselves to new areas of interest that give us deeper insights and greater perspectives, which, in turn, create an inner peace and make us wiser.

For happy old men, what matters is attaining a balance and greater perspectives, both into oneself and the world. It's no longer about learning for life but rather about living in the moment. It's important to live life to the fullest, every step of the way. It's about shooting for the stars and landing somewhere in the middle. We won't leave any unlived life behind when we're gone. And I want to do less now in order to achieve more.

THE MAN WHO turns sixty-five today can count on living another eighteen years. This means most of us can hope to be quite old. For many, the years between sixty-five and eighty are the best of their lives. After that, real old age begins. This means that we have a lot to look forward to.

Getting older involves transitioning from one stage to another, from self to soul, and attaining some fraction of wisdom. You lose one thing, but win another.

Wisdom does not automatically come with age. You have to search for it yourself, in philosophy, in nature, in fine art, or in religion. It's not about training or education anymore, but about cultivation and balance. Don't forget that life is short, but art is long, as the Romans said.

By looking at oneself from the viewpoint of eternity, we all become contemporaries and can socialize with Homer and Montaigne on equal footing. Our circle of friends expands precisely in that instant in which our friends begin to depart. This makes the last stretch easier to travel.

MAN IS THE only living organism that is conscious of its own ultimate death. Many of us find that unnerving. But man is also the only living organism with a sense of humor, able to laugh at itself. This makes everything considerably easier.

For our entire lives, our mortality drives us to act—this notion of wanting to really do something with the only life we get. What's important, then, is to avoid dying while we go on living, and to actually be alive when we die. It's not over until the end.

Concrete advice isn't always enough. We need the support of those who have lived before us and who have developed worldviews that can comfort us and cheer us. For this reason, I have collected 109 comforting thoughts for the continuing journey here, in *Older and Wiser*. Now, it's all about celebrating each happy day, and forgetting the rest!

The meaning of life most likely cannot be found in science or religion. We have to find it within ourselves. Different people find different meanings at different times. My own ethos consists of a bit of everything I've picked up along the way: snippets and words of wisdom built on my own experiences and the experiences of others. In this field, there are no experts. Your thoughts are worth just as much as mine.

"WHERE SCIENCE ENDS, spirituality begins!" said Albert Einstein.

I find that to be comforting.

"I have occasionally thought rather deeply, though seldom with pleasure, almost always unwillingly, and as if forced to do so," said the French philosopher Rousseau.

I agree with that.

What matters now is to make the best of life while we still have time here on Earth.

NOW IT'S NO longer about our free time— rather, it's about all the time we have left, every bit of it free time. As retirees, seniors, old men, geriatrics, or elderly folk, we've gone from working life to limitless vacation. This is actually quite a bit of time we're talking about—and a lot to look forward to. You might even call it a sort of harvest.

This isn't an easy transition for everyone. A large portion of our lives has been spent focusing on planning, competing, and moving forward, but seldom on enjoying our accomplishments. Demands, both others' and our own, have dominated our time, and everyone is not fully happy with the results. Many have consoled themselves with lies and wishful thinking. Nobody makes it through life unscathed. And now we're standing here without a fixed agenda, with more time than we've ever had before.

The great turning point, now that we can choose for ourselves, is that we can create a new life before death. This is what the new freedom is about.

ONE TYPICALLY FIGURES that a third of all retired men are happy, a third are unhappy, and a third are resigned to their fate. The resigned ones have it the worst. Some can still be woken up by a eureka moment. The unhappy ones are more actively focused, and thus willing to change their lives—if they haven't locked themselves into hopeless defensive positions, of course, which is something quite a few older folks do.

To be more content with life, we have to do away with any lingering grief and look on the lives we have made with a sense of satisfaction.

Of course, you may have run into bad luck, but as a rule, you've had a hand in how it all turned out. That's why deep inside ourselves, we know very well why things are the way they are, which ought to help us understand ourselves and how to change.

All of this assumes that we take a sort of trip within ourselves to find out who we really are, and what we want out of the rest of life. In many cases, this means finding new insights and experiences. Life becomes even longer if we fill it with exciting things. Being active, in and of itself, means that in turn more new and unique things will happen to us.

In old age, we have to continue to look forward and engage ourselves with the future. But we don't need to have a guilty conscience anymore, or try to engage ourselves in everything. It's time to sleep well at night, after all. Now, with a clean conscience, we can see and hear only what we want to.

MODERN PEOPLE REQUIRE more from life, more than ever before. We older folk should do the same. Here's what one modern psychologist has written:

"Don't accept an existence that looks a bit gray. You can require more from life—that it be fun and that it quicken your pulse. This is a personal responsibility that every human being has."

You could say the same thing in the words of Karlsson-on-the-Roof, the titular character of a series of Swedish children's books by Astrid Lindgren: "I want fun and games, laughs and shenanigans; or else, I want no part of this."

A HEALTHY BRAIN has high plasticity and continues to renew itself even in later years. The activity in an active retiree's brain resembles the brain activity of younger people, according to one study. A twenty-year-old and an eighty-year-old can be on an equal playing field when competing to solve the same kinds of mental challenges. On the other hand, an eighty-year-old cannot run as fast as a twenty-year-old. So let's focus on our comparative advantages!

We also tend to overlook the fact that forgetting details has its advantages, namely the ability to see the big picture. This is really something to seize hold of! So we have nothing to complain about. No, we needn't pity the human race, as Swedish author August Strindberg claimed. Not yet—and not for you and me, at any rate.

At one point in time, people stood right in the midst of life until they died. Death was a public concern. But with the advent of a fixed retirement age in the latter half of the twentieth century, a greater distance grew between our public selves and our private deaths. It is this part that we will now fill with happiness and meaning. Here, the old expression "I've retired to a private life" fits like a glove.

AT ONE PERIOD in history, moments of happiness were more the exception than the rule. Life consisted of illness and misfortune that smote young and old, rich and poor. Disappointment was a natural part of life. Most people lived with some sort of chronic pain. They had no choice but to bite the bullet and keep on going. There was no giving up, and many lived off of hope.

In the olden days, religion was a consolation. The worse off you were here on Earth, the better you'd have it in heaven—in the afterlife. Today, many of us demand the kingdom of heaven right here on Earth and are easily disappointed when society does not deliver.

In the Western world, we've grown comfortable and used to a life without significant material challenges. Perhaps we'd be better off if we were a bit more conscious of life's ups and downs. The foremost benefit of such an outlook would be that we would really appreciate and delight in the good things that happen to us. Gratitude is the heart's way of remembering.

We can't forget that happiness is nearly always a byproduct of the life we live every day. In that respect, each and every one of us has his own responsibility. When you yourself actually take hold of life, the lump in your chest is released too, and the emptiness in your soul is filled. Life is endlessly more interesting than death.

Sometimes, we are inescapably bored, but this too has its value:

"Indeed, through boredom, one can learn much about oneself," said the Swedish poet Gunnar Ekelöf, while listless adolescents often wonder, "Is there a life before death?" There are perspectives that divide us by age.

BEING A RETIREE is like riding a bike. If you're bored, you'll feel like you're riding a stationary exercise bike. But if you're having fun, you'll find yourself on an exciting adventure. You are the one who sets the pace.

109 thoughts for the continuing journey

1

MOST OF IT IS CRAP

Occasionally, I will hear old men say this. No, actually, it's not. You just have to open your eyes and count your blessings. All that glitters is gold when you get older—just like when we were little boys. The little boy is still alive in the happy old man; indeed, the child is the father of the man, as they say.

So get going and don't wait any longer; only you know what you really want to do. We've retired from our jobs, not from life.

"As long as there's life, there's hope," one proverb says.

There are no cul-de-sacs in life. You just have to find the crossing, take a shortcut, jump, or continue right on. That's how I got to be a happy old man. Each one of us decides how the journey will continue. Don't let your past dictate the rest of your life. And consider that certain things are best left undone.

Don't make it any more complicated than it has to be. Sometimes, all it takes is walking your dog or sitting down with a newspaper and a cup of coffee, in peace and quiet.

"It's nice to get old. Being young was bloody awful."

Swedish author HJALMAR SÖDERBERG

2

IT'S NEVER TOO LATE

"I'm seventy years old," I heard someone say. "It's too late for me to change my life."

No, it's never too late; but, of course, you can't live the same way you did when you were younger. I recently attended a gala dinner in New York, when someone said in a speech: "As is so often said: Age is a matter of mind. And if you don't mind, it doesn't matter."

No, there is no road back—but there are several different paths forward. The Greek philosopher Socrates learned to dance and play the cittern in his sixties (2500 years ago). So don't wait for the perfect moment, as the perfect moment is never going to come.

"On s'engage, et puis on voit." You get started and then you see, as Napoleon said. Or as United Nations mediator Hans Blix said on his eighty-fifth birthday: "I've retired so many times that I don't intend to do it again."

Each day carries the future in its womb. As the proverb goes, "No person is so old that she can no longer learn." So seize the day! Carpe diem! A wise exhortation from the Roman poet Horatius.

3

THE SWEDES ARE SET TO HAVE THE LONGEST LIFE EXPECTANCY IN THE WORLD

Recently, there have been news stories about how the Swedes have the longest life expectancy. We have long known that there are certain places in the world where one can live a better, healthier life and become quite old, such as the Caucasus. But it was perhaps news for most of us that the Swedish province of Småland is also one such place, and that Markaryd County is its epicenter. I don't think I've ever heard a better argument for moving somewhere!

The rest of us can console ourselves with the Roman philosopher Seneca's words: "What's important is not how long you live, but how well you live."

4

ABOUT THE WORTH OF OLD PEOPLE

"If old things are so valuable, why aren't old people the same?" one of my grandchildren asked. I can only smile. This is the big question and in this regard, people in the East and the West have completely different ideas.

Young Chinese people ask their elders, "How great is your awe-inspiring age?" while our elderly do everything they can to hide their age.

But can one become wise without becoming old? "Youth has a fair face; old age, a beautiful soul," says a Swedish proverb, many years old though it may be. As Cicero wrote: "Everyone wants to live long, but no one wants to be old."

Already in Spain, things are better: "retiring" is called jubilación and "retired" is jubilado. Doesn't it sound wonderful?

Personally, I'm striving to become a part of the new, trendy group called FOP: Fabulous Older People.

5

WE'LL DO THAT IN OUR NEXT LIFE

That's what my wife and I tell each other when we've found yet another thing we want to do before life is over. It sounds cheery, and is a lovely way of saying that there's only a short time left to live, and that it's important to choose and concentrate on certain things, do them properly and well, and leave the rest for, well, your next life.

Occasionally I'm compelled to use the phrase "in my previous life" to cover up the years that disappeared without a trace in my first marriage. If it's not one thing, it's the other.

6

ILLNESS GIVES US INSIGHT INTO THE TRUE VALUE OF LIFE

"Life has been good to me!" is something I often say, as that's how I've experienced things ever since I began counting my blessings. "But aren't you forgetting all your illnesses, the cancer, your heart, your hip?"

No, I'm not. These ailments gave me new insight into life's true value, and the willpower to keep from giving up. He who has never been sick has yet to get to know himself.

"There are two ways to live life," said Albert Einstein. "One as if nothing is a miracle and one as if everything is."

And all you have to do is choose.

7

LAUGHTER
LENGTHENS LIFE

Recently, I was sitting on the commuter train with two older women I didn't know opposite me.

"I didn't know if I should laugh or cry," one said to the other.

"In that case, I think it'd be best to laugh," I said.

There was a second of silence after this unexpected contribution from a stranger.

Then, all three of us laughed.

"The absurd act, rebellion, is man's constant presence in himself."

French author ALBERT CAMUS

8

TO FEEL AWE

One gray January day in the 1960s, I read the following lines in *The Man Without Qualities* by Austrian author Robert Musil:

"And suddenly, the double doors to the study open, and outside I see the endless sea, lapping at my threshold."

That made me shudder.

This image has never ceased to fascinate me, as it gave me a sudden glimpse of how it could be to feel awe—to stand alone before God, as it was once called.

For two years of my life, I participated in major international political events. I was the Swedish Consul General in Leningrad, Tallinn, Riga, and Vilnius when communism collapsed in the USSR, and Estonia, Latvia, and Lithuania liberated themselves from the Soviet occupation forces.

Every morning when I woke, I felt awe. The events I took part in were much greater than I and my little family, and they were the greatest to occur in the realm of Swedish foreign policy during our lifetime. It was as if two pieces of continental shelf crashed into each other. Sweden could just as well have been crushed, for none could know if or when the Red Army or the secret police, the KGB, would strike back.

9

MAKE PEACE WITH YOURSELF

Over the course of our lives, we've needed to build up many myths about ourselves in order to handle adversity and setbacks, to create incentive and trust. Now, the time has come to disband these myths so that they no longer haunt our dreams. Be honest with yourself—it's remarkably freeing.

Jealousy, anger, and grief take away life's freshness and color and cause it to wither. I'm not saying you should distance yourself from your earlier life, but that you should change the way you live right now, for example, by socializing with friends who make you happier and are more fun to be around. So let's be a bit more generous to ourselves, and look at our problems with a light, positive attitude. This makes them easier to solve.

Besides, happier people have happier friends and acquaintances. It's easier to live with a happy old man than a bitter one. Don't forget that optimists can live a whole seven years longer and happier than pessimists.

Everything leans toward giving it a try!

10

MAKE PEACE WITH OTHERS

As we age, it's important to put old conflicts behind us and reconcile with those who can still be reconciled with. The older we get, the more ludicrous it becomes to place all the blame on our deceased parents, for instance. Your parents weren't perfect, and if you have children of your own, you probably weren't perfect either. After a long life, we know how difficult it is to keep many balls in the air at the same time. Some fall to the ground; others don't.

The Swedish botanist Carl von Linné kept a notebook he called *Nemesis Divina*—God's Vengeance. In it, he meticulously recorded when the good lord would smite his enemies with illness, adversity, and death.

Keeping such a log is not a good idea.

Repressed conflict often leads to tension that raises one's blood pressure and weakens the immune system. And so, making peace with yourself is also a question of health. Let bygones be bygones.

Reconciliation does not require you to take up old injustices and dwell on them again, but instead asks you to recognize each other's past experiences as legitimate. And then move on.

It's worth noting that we can also be reconciled to those who have died by gradually changing the way we think about them. We can do this by making space for them in our minds, from which he or she has long been barred.

It's a process that will do you a lot of good; I can attest to that personally.

11

STRIVE FOR WISDOM

The one thing we ought to strive for as older people is a pinch of wisdom. Wisdom is the only thing that can give us insights that make the last years worth living. Wisdom is the only thing that can diminish our fear of death.

Wisdom involves a process of liberation from that which is insignificant, and a concentration on that which is significant—a movement from body to soul, from "myself" to the big picture and the lengthy perspectives of time.

It's about placing your life within a larger story, which gives meaning and satisfaction. Now we can find the red thread running through our experience and, in turn, find our real, true selves. The puzzle pieces finally fall into place.

This requires the courage not to be remarkable, but to simply be yourself. Lose the prestige—it is a useful exercise.

12

"YOU'RE ONE OF THOSE DAMN *HAPPY* PEOPLE, AREN'T YOU?"

I've heard these words many times since my previous book *Older and Happier!* was published.

And no, I'm not one of those irritatingly cheery people—I think you know who I mean—but I have been working on a lot about myself in recent years. The advantage to being conscious of and making demands of oneself is that I now always know when I fail. When I do, I've got to pick myself up once more and start all over again.

It's better to expect a lot from yourself and fail than to expect nothing at all.

In the olden days, humans were afraid of God's judgment. Today, we're more afraid of the judgments of our peers: Am I good enough? Is my job good enough?

God judges, men condemn. The questions multiply, and they invite worry and unease.

13

LIFE IS LIKE A DANCE

Wisdom doesn't come automatically with age, especially not in our youth-obsessed, news-oriented, and trend-sensitive society. Wisdom requires you to cultivate your soul a bit more and to let go of some of your body's demands—that is quite the opposite of today's flighty ideals. It requires more of an immersion into the humanities, so that the soul receives nourishment, and our experiences gain structure and perspective.

It is here that art, literature, music, and religion get their revenge, as they deal ultimately with the human condition and one's place in life.

Wisdom also demands that you think a bit less about yourself. Doing so is also freeing: it silences the inner voice, our constant companion with its eternal nagging, and we can live experiences to the fullest. At its best, life is like a dance: we enjoy the movement and have fun, but we don't actually get anywhere.

That right there is happiness. But as always, it's also about daring to lead.

14

WISDOM IS ITS
OWN REWARD

Wisdom frees us from the rush of keeping up, from the pressure to learn about all the latest trends, from engaging in yet another conflict, either at home or out in the world at large. Old, wise men don't rush into things blindly, and they don't walk straight into walls and become burned-out cases.

Wisdom also allows us a bit of laziness after a long life. It lets us feel the satisfaction of being finished with the day's work. It lets us feel the joy in simply digging in the garden or meditating in the sunset. Ram-tam tam tiddel-am, as Winnie the Pooh would say. Sit under the palaver tree, as my Kenyan friends would say.

"I feel a bit tired now—pleasantly tired," said Canadian author Alice Munro when she received her 2013 Nobel Prize.

It's easy to recognize yourself in her words. All too often, we chase after air and caw into the wind. It is first in silence that we are able to grasp the meaning of the words. Wisdom demands that you are comfortable in your own company.

Each and every one of us must find wisdom in his own way. Here are two ways that fit me perfectly:

> "I sought peace in wisdom,
> but found oblivion in nature."
> Russian author ALEKSEY TOLSTOY

> "You ask for a miracle—
> and yet you don't see the sunset."
> German poet J. W. GOETHE

And best of all: nature is always open.

15

LOOK OUT FOR THE ARROGANCE OF OLD AGE

"It's nice to know that you're always right," an old woman said during dinner one evening.

We all fell silent.

If you see yourself as the only one who knows anything, the only one who understands, the only wise one, your situation can become quite dangerous. Try to prevent this from developing over time by not always basing everything on your own experience. Be sure to listen without judging and condemning, and don't be afraid or unsettled by the new or unknown.

"You don't have to eat it all, but you have to taste it," we always told our kids when they were little.

It's the same with old folks, too.

"Let's not argue about facts," my American friends say. And it's true. These days, all one needs to do is take out a mobile phone and Google something to get a quick overview of the facts and avoid pointless bickering. In that respect, technological developments have completely changed the rules of the game. It's become increasingly difficult to paint yourself into a corner. That's good news for us older people.

16

WITH EACH PASSING YEAR, WE BECOME MORE AND MORE ALONE

If we choose this for ourselves, it's fine. Otherwise, it can be burdensome. Personally, I've been lucky. I was an only child, but I married into a large family with lots of brothers and sisters, children and grandchildren. Today, there's a lot of hubbub around me. I like that—as long as I'm left in peace!

17

CALMING DOWN DOES US ALL GOOD

Your heart works hard for your entire life without ever getting a break. Your brain cells transmit their impulses at a speed of about 185 miles per hour. No wonder your thoughts flit about, your heart pounds and your mouth gasps at times.

Do this experiment the next time someone dwells on their problems with you. Ask them directly: "Do you have a concrete problem right now?" Ninety-five percent of the time, the answer will be evasive. Once you get that out of the way, the two of you can unwind and enjoy a pleasant evening together with other, more enjoyable things to talk about.

From my years spent in Russia, I have fond memories of the old Russian custom of always sitting down together for a short time before someone leaves. For a moment, time stops. Suddenly, we're all sitting there in the hall, in Anton Chekhov's *The Cherry Orchard* or in our home in St. Petersburg, simply being quiet and reflecting together.

This is an agreeable change of pace that triggers feelings of peace and fellowship. The heart and brain, too, get a chance to unwind.

"The slower you go, the farther you will come," says a Russian proverb. There's wisdom in old proverbs and traditions like this one.

18

CHAOS IS GOD'S NEIGHBOR

But for many of us, it's not enough to attain wisdom. We want consolation, too. That's why religion plays such an important role. In our specialized society, the church has become a specialist for souls. There is much that's transitory, and so it can feel safe and secure to stick to old lessons—lessons that are unquestionable because they stand outside of the world of reason. That which religious people call prayer and which atheists call a security blanket is often what I would call meditation. It can be good for that inner calm that we all need so much.

But the line between consolation and self-righteousness is thin. The greater part of human evil comes from people who are convinced that their own judgments are correct, and all others are wrong. Paradoxically enough, the greater a role religion is allowed to play in a society, the stronger the hate culture will grow. We need only to think of the religious wars in the 1600s or follow the news on the radio and TV to get some formidable examples from our own time.

"God is dead!" many shouted alongside the German philosopher Nietzsche in the 1900s. I myself am not so sure anymore, but that is likely more as a means to guard myself, not tactically, but simply because I really just do not know. When it comes to faith and metaphysics, there's no room for absolute certainty. But personally, I prefer lukewarm Christianity to burning fanaticism.

The border between science and faith is constantly shifting. In the summer of 2012, researchers at the particle physics laboratory at CERN in Geneva reported that it was believed the so-called Higgs boson had been discovered, also called the "God particle,"—the one responsible for the "Big Bang" that was behind the creation of the universe, and ultimately, the creation of humankind.

Life is truly amazing!

19

PHILOSOPHY IS A WAY OF THINKING

Philosophy is not something you can plug into. Philosophy is a way of thinking and asking questions so that, hopefully, you learn something. Greek philosopher Socrates is said to be the first philosopher in the history of the West because as he walked the streets of Athens in the 400s BC, he asked the question of how men can live good lives.

The answer lies in the realm of the Forms, said his student, Plato, who founded a school he called the Academy.

"No, the answer is to be found in the natural world around us," replied Plato's student, Aristotle, from his own school, the Lyceum.

I believe in Aristotle more than in Plato, but perhaps I believe most in Nietzsche. It is our mind's reality that matters, and the great battle in life is, according to Nietzsche, the one against our own inertia—against sloth and passivity. It is only after this fight is won that we gain power over our true selves, and the strength to withstand suffering, and the capacity to delight in life. This is empowerment, and everyone ought to get a hold of it. This is when you become a happy old man in the truest sense.

An old Swedish proverb sums up the question: "True wisdom is knowing that you know nothing." Truly in the spirit of Socrates!

It is also believed that Socrates once said: "How many things I can do without!" It was wise then, it is wise now.

20

LEARN FROM EPICURUS

The prominent Greek stoic Epicurus established his own school called the Garden, where all were welcome to sit down and enjoy life and our sprouting friends. His basic philosophy was to live simply but well, to enjoy the company of others and forget all cares. There's no sense in getting worked up about something we cannot change.

Epicurus also considered old age to be the apex of life, something important to take advantage of and enjoy. It's more important to eat in good company than to eat good food. True friendship assumes that one looks for nothing in the other, save for friendship itself. This is a goal in and of itself, and a foundation for good conversation.

Stoicism, in principle, is based on the idea of preserving one's peace in all situations by accepting that there is much we can't do anything about and so there is no point wasting time on it. The road to this internal tranquility passes through a lack of desires and independence from all external conditions. Then, we arrive at peace.

All were welcome in Epicurus's garden—men and women, regardless of social status, as long as they wanted to learn. Doesn't that sound ideal?

Here's how I'd like to see my own garden: roses, apple trees, a cup of tea, a good book, my wife, my daughters, a friend, a glass of wine, and finally a nap. I'd have everything I need right there.

Epicurus wasn't afraid of death, either: "As long as we live, death is not here, and when death comes, we won't be here any longer." With Stoicism, one avoids monotheistic religion's absurd pretenses of possessing the only real truth, which has created so much misfortune in the world.

Welcome to my garden!

21

IMMERSE YOURSELF IN THE FINE ARTS

Seeing as none of us is in possession of the truth about life and death, art, music, and literature can be very helpful and consoling. Perhaps it is for this reason we call them the "fine arts." Here, we deal in cultivation of the mind rather than book learning, the ability to feel joy and see the big picture. For many of us, this can become our grand project in our later days.

All those who have lived before us have had similar experiences, and some have immortalized these experiences in artistic, musical, and literary works. They can help us to see ourselves in a broader context, which is the first step on the path toward wisdom. Surely there's more to life than booze, sex, and money, as the media constantly tells us.

"He who cannot see himself in a sphere of at least two thousand others is shackled for his whole life, both by day and night," wrote the German poet Rainer Maria Rilke.

"I write for that part of me that I have in common with other people," wrote Swedish poet Gunnar Ekelöf.

That's how a real humanist talks.

22

THE WHOLE IS GREATER THAN THE SUM OF ITS PARTS

As time goes on, so too does life, and with each passing generation the human race becomes progressively better adapted to the conditions of the future. I can see that my children are cleverer than I am when it comes to most things. The digital divide is somewhere around the age of fifty today. Even though they have our genes and were raised by us, our children have a freer, broader outlook on most questions than we do, which makes room for new thoughts and approaches. Hopefully, they've taken away the best of us.

One generation stands on the shoulders of the previous. The whole is often greater than the sum of its parts, thankfully.

With each new generation, society rids itself of more and more prejudices and narrow-mindedness left over from earlier epochs. This is really rather fortunate; how else would we phase out old Nazis and communists from previous decades?

23

OUR VALUES SHIFT

Each generation focuses on its own set of values. A recent study found that the top five values up to this point are:

1. Health   2. World peace   3. Honesty
4. Freedom   5. Familial security

are diminishing in popularity, while the five new values growing most rapidly are:

1. A comfortable life   2. A life full of enjoyment
3. An exciting life   4. Equality
5. Wisdom—finally, there it is!

24

OUR WORLDVIEW
IS OUTDATED

I went to school from 1951 to 1963. Almost nothing I learned then is still current. Julius Caesar and I had more in common than I do with today's schoolchildren. I belong to the last generation that read his *The Gallic Wars* in the original Latin.

Our worldview was shaped by the Cold War, and the fall of the USSR was our generation's significant event; I was lucky enough to be right there for that one, living in Russia at that time. But this also means that, today, my picture of the world is at least twenty-five years too old.

But what happened to our dreams, then? Most of them didn't become reality; for example, I never became a streetcar conductor in Uppsala, nor a senator in the American Congress. But I became so much else instead, just like you did.

"Life is what happens while you are making other plans," as John Lennon sang.

25

OUR CHILDREN AND GRANDCHILDREN ARE MEETING A DIFFERENT SOCIETY

We Baby Boomers grew up in a society that was stable and homogenous. Our children and grandchildren are meeting an entirely different society and must be prepared for it. Our realities are worlds apart. No wonder the gap between generations is getting wider.

While we admittedly no longer share the same future, we can still share the same present. I like to keep that in mind.

One thing I do know, though, is that it is unacceptable for the media to try to lump together us older white men and portray us as non-persons and exclude us from the societal community. It's reminiscent of Stalin's method of labeling people from before the revolution as "former human beings."

But I accept the challenge!

This is why the distance between generations sometimes feels far and foreign, especially if we think that we still know best and that we still know the most. The best we can do is to keep our curiosity alive and stay "with it" for as long as we can; in short, surprise the younger generations with new ideas. This is the only way we can get "cred" in their eyes.

Striving toward yourself

26

NEVER FORGET THAT THERE IS MUCH TO BE JOYFUL ABOUT

Take a look at yourself in the mirror and look on the bright side!

There you are, you meet your face—the part of your body that has met the world over all these years and that carries traces of all those encounters. Now in the mirror, I see an older man who has lived a good life together with a delightful woman, with whom he has energetic children, and with whom he has eaten lots of good food and drank lots of good Burgundy wine. Every lost hair, every wrinkle—or are those racing stripes?—is a memory from a long, good life.

Indeed, life is not only a game, but also a bed of roses, as the weekly papers wrote in our youth. You both can and should see it that way—for your own sake.

When I see myself in a hospital mirror, I like to raise my hand in greeting and say, "Hey you, old friend, here we are again!" or "Let's have another go!" A day without a smile is a wasted day.

With a bit of imagination, I can also glimpse the final old geezer I'm eventually going to become. It fills me with fear-tinged anticipation. My greatest fear is the thought of becoming a boring grandfather to my own grandchildren, too old and listless to handle a three-year-old as fast as quicksilver.

27

YOU CAN CONTINUE TO DEVELOP FOR AS LONG AS YOU LIVE

This is, in fact, a prerequisite to life itself. You don't need to be on the front lines anymore, but you can't just fall back on clichés. Always think before uttering objections or criticism. A good question to ask yourself in such cases is:

"Do you really think that, or is that just one of the many clichés that circulate among old people? And if you do think that, do you really need to say it?"

It has taken me almost my entire lifetime to learn that hearing what others have to say is more interesting than what I myself say. Though my wife would add that I've yet to be completely convinced.

28

WITH EACH GENERATION, WE OLDER FOLK HAVE GOTTEN YOUNGER

Perhaps this is small consolation. But there's a limit we can't exceed. Thankfully, none of us actually know where it is, so we can only hope. Not everything is good to know.

I, for example, do not ever intend to get tested to see if I am predisposed to Alzheimer's disease, simply because my father died in that horrendous manner. I'm hard-pressed to come up with a better way to disrupt the joy of life than to find out my fate. There's no cure, anyway.

I would rather be blissfully ignorant until it strikes.

29

SEX?

Just because we feel young doesn't
automatically mean we're younger in every way.
Speaking strictly physically, there's a lot that
happens that can be hard to deal with as we get
older.

My advice is to keep your long-term,
established relationship alive and well, as
intimacy and trust are important for keeping
your love life in working order. There's a lot of
power in the fidelity behind a long-standing
romance, so stay in the same bed in the same
room. Faithfulness is important when we start

to become frail and need support to keep on going. The loyalty of love is the first buoy in old age.

It's important to maintain your integrity. The media constantly goes on about the sexualization of society, but that's not for everyone. Each of us has his own superego, and his own private parts. And everything has its time. It can, on the other hand, be restful to let sexuality subside. Don't forget that old age is friendship's golden age, which also means a great deal of intimacy. Eros becomes Agape.

Women seem to be defined more by their sex than men are. For many women, menopause is an opportunity to "take the step over to the third gender," to cite the French writer Simone de Beauvoir, and to create for oneself a new freedom between gender boundaries. This is a freedom most men have had all along, if they so chose. It's never too late to become the family's favorite uncle.

I remember a novel I read when I was young. A young man is sitting on a bus in Italy when a colorful, yet decrepit woman gets on. The young man turns to her for a lack of other female company, but she puts him in his place immediately, pointing to her nether regions and saying: "Now that devil's finally dead!"

30

THINGS DIDN'T USED TO BE BETTER

Two hundred years ago, Sweden was a poor country in Europe, and the Swedes were among the poorest people in Europe. The mortality rate was high, and diseases were fuelled by insatiable alcohol consumption.

Today, we have a hard time grasping the concept that a man in his fifties could already be on his last legs. But back then, men were worn out after long lives of drinking, debauchery, and STDs. The Swedes have never drunk as much as they did during the late 1700s—ten times more than today. And never since have as many illegitimate children been born. Family life was disintegrating among all social groups, and violence was common. Many were struck down in dark alleys, and the elderly didn't dare go out.

Doesn't that sound familiar?

Nothing is new under the stars.

31

THE ZEITGEIST IS CONSTANTLY DOING FLIPS AND THE PENDULUM SWINGS

But soon, young Victoria would ascend the throne of Great Britain, and a new world would be born with Christian revivalism and a growing temperance movement. Eventually, even pantalettes would be placed over the legs of furniture to discourage immoral thoughts.

This is what we call the pendulum swings of time, and these are both fascinating and completely unpredictable. It is the zeitgeist that causes a whole generation to dance to its own rhythm, from the isolationism in America in the

1920s and thirties to the leftist movement in the 1970s.

The question is which way will the winds blow next time? There are always new, unexpected factors that trigger these changes. Perhaps it's time for a bit more religion and neomoralism? In that case, liquor and pornography will likely be condemned, and nightclubs will be closed. Private morals will probably be a public matter once more, and many will be forced back into their homes—and into the closets.

It has been this way throughout history. Perhaps the clock will again move from 12 to 1, as it has so often done in the past.

32

BECOMING OLD IS UP TO YOU

Medical research points to evidence that genes affect about 25 percent of the conditions of our aging; the environment, another 25 percent; and the lifestyle we choose, the remaining 50 percent. In other words, we are the ones who provide the framework within which our genes have their influence. A British study has attempted to categorize the various factors that affect one's lifespan in terms of plus and minus. Here are some encouraging examples:

• One drink a day, or two glasses of wine, will prolong your life by about thirty minutes each time. But if you double your intake of alcohol, you shorten your life by an hour per each drink or two glasses of wine.

• Two cups of coffee per day prolongs your life by thirty minutes per cup; more cups reduce it!

• If you exercise for twenty minutes a day, you get an extra hour of life each time. This is a fantastic exchange rate!

• But if you eat 3 ounces (85 grams) of red meat daily, your life will be shortened by thirty minutes each time.

• If you sit down in front of the TV for two hours a day, you'll cut an additional thirty minutes off your life each time.

• Smoking is a guaranteed fast track to death: a pack of cigarettes shortens your life by five (!) hours.

Doctors are currently mulling over the fact that mortality rates have declined so sharply for our seventy-year-olds. It seems more and more of them are living to be eighty plus. Are the Baby Boomers once again trying to defy gravity by living healthily?

33

WE CAN ACTUALLY
BECOME TOO OLD

"Are you Ingrid Tham's daughter?" asked
an old woman at the table in the assisted living
facility where I was drinking coffee with my
eighty-four-year-old mother. Mom looked upward
questioningly.

"I was a classmate of your mother's," the
woman explained.

I was taken aback. This was my grandmother
she was talking about, born in the 1800s, and
mother to my old mother who sat beside me.
Everything swam before my eyes.

It turned out that the old lady was 104
years old! Here we were, three generations of
old people, drinking coffee. At home, we had

children and grandchildren. Five generations, all alive at the same time.

To continue complaining about how short life is after this experience would have been absurd. But this is hardly the first time such a thing has happened, if we are to believe the book of Job in the Bible: "Job lived for 140 years and got to see his children and grandchildren through four generations."

We'll have to stop in Markaryd next time and take a deep breath.

After we finished our coffee, Mom gave me a list of seven errands she wanted me to take care of in different parts of the city.

"But Mom, I'm old. I don't have the energy for all of this!" I answered despairingly.

She looked at me with disbelief: her old son. To our parents, we always remain children, the little people whose bottoms they once powdered.

So at last, we must die—for our children's sake.

Thank
goodness for
forgetfulness

34

A POOR MEMORY IS AN IMPORTANT PART OF BEING A HAPPY OLD MAN

It's too soon to begin living in the past. That's why we've got to continue forgetting in order to keep moving on in life. We have to concentrate on remembering the fun, happy times and forgetting all the failures and worries. My mother complained about my memory already years ago:

"You always make things so easy for yourself."

"Yeah, I suppose I do."

That was the whole point, I thought.

When we get to be properly old, however, we'll remember everything that we forgot we remembered, too. As long as we still remember our memory!

35

WHEN THE NAME DISAPPEARS 'ROUND THE CORNER

Sometimes I experience, in a visceral way, how the process of forgetting takes place. When I forget a name, it's as if the name, just like a squirrel's tail, disappears as it rounds the corner of a hotel hallway, and the last thing I see is the big, reddish-brown tail as I hear an echo of the forgotten name resounding in my ears. It's rather exasperating.

What does the goddess of memory, Mnemosyne, have to say about that?

36

WHEN FORGETFULNESS STRIKES

Every senior knows the fear associated with the idea of losing one's memory, and we're constantly on guard, watching for any lapses. We've got our brains on the brain, you might say. Forgetting names and details is totally natural. Otherwise, in our age, our memories would flood their banks. This kind of forgetfulness is good.

A study shows that the risk of memory loss decreases by 50 percent if we do physical exercise regularly. This, of course, is something we can do on our own, which means that we're not helpless victims to the process of forgetting. That's important to know.

Forgetting also causes us to lose valuable time from what's left of our lives. Another study shows that old people lose up to a month every year in time spent searching for telephone numbers, names, keys, glasses, and so on.

I remember an older acquaintance in New York who told me that he was out walking in Central Park one day when he saw an elegant woman he recognized, but whose name he had forgotten. He walked up to her and greeted her, wondering if they hadn't met before.

"We certainly have—we were married at one point," she replied sourly. These are what we call "senior moments."

I walk out into the kitchen and suddenly stop. I no longer remember why I went there. This is nothing to be worried about; everybody else does it too. But if you stand in the kitchen and don't know what kind of room you're in . . . that's when you've got yourself a problem.

37

WE ALL REMEMBER SUCH DIFFERENT THINGS

Meetings with old classmates can have an unexpected effect, since we each remember such different things. A few years ago, I met an old classmate from secondary school. We hadn't ever been close, and we made some small talk about our time in school, when he suddenly cut me off by saying:

"I've got to tell you something. I'm never going to forget the time when you came to our class from America and you got to tell us what it was like going to an American school. You went to the front of the class and sat down behind the teacher's desk, as calmly and easily as the headmaster himself, and told us without any hesitation about fantastic things we had never heard of before. We didn't believe our ears! You painted a picture of a different, fascinating life. Yes, you really came as a breath of fresh air in our class."

I have seldom been so amazed, as these were dark years in my life. My memories of that time are filled with angst.

This meeting prompted me to realize that we go about our lives with tunnel vision, without understanding what other people think and feel. We're like trains meeting in the night: a sudden light, a whistle, and then it's dark once again.

It wasn't for naught that British foreign minister Duff Cooper called his memoir *Old Men Forget*. It's a shame the title's already taken—but I'll forget it soon enough.

38

MAY HE LIVE FOR MANY HUNDRED YEARS!

The number of centenarians is growing dramatically—among men, too. In Sweden, all of those who turn one hundred receive birthday greetings from His Majesty King Carl XVI Gustaf. A moment of excitement, for what it's worth.

Old scientists can console themselves with the fact that they reach the element with the atomic number seventy-nine gold, when they turn seventy-nine. At eighty they reach mercury (quicksilver), and at ninety-two uranium. Not bad. But eighty-two must feel rather heavy: lead.

When we get to be good and really old, we will instead find joy in all of our unbirthdays, to quote Pippi Longstocking. The number of remaining real birthdays is quite simply too low by then.

Considering how long we are all living these days, Sweden's traditional birthday song's "Yea, may he live a hundred years" may seem a bit on the stingy side. I've seen a lot of stiffened smiles in such situations. Instead, I prefer to sing "Yea, may he live many hundred years." With every passing year, we outlive more and more people. When we eventually die, our individual lives will have lasted as long as many eras in history. Democracy lasted 110 years in Athens, and democracy in Sweden has lasted for ninety years so far.

We can beat that!

39

THERE'S NOTHING WRONG WITH BEING A LATE BLOOMER

My motto is: "It's never too late." I have always been a late bloomer. As a kid I probably seemed rather sluggish at times. But now, late blooming is quite the right approach. A late bloomer always has something new left to delight in. Slow and steady wins the race.

What, you don't mean we're already there?

I have pursued a career as a children's author in my older days. To date, I have written twelve books since leaving diplomacy. I don't want to be a public figure anymore—I want to do things for myself during the last lap. But I'm still a man of the future, so look out—here I come on the inside track! Sometimes it feels like life really wants us to succeed!

Indeed, possessing a child's spirit is a dream for a children's book writer.

40

DON'T LET BEING SICK TURN INTO A FULL-TIME JOB

Many older people worry about their health so much that it becomes an obstacle to living a good life. Sickness should not be allowed to take over our lives and become a full-time job. Watch out if you start finding yourself at the pharmacy more often than the liquor store!

41

DON'T JUST LET TIME PASS

When we get older, there's a risk that everything will simply keep rolling along, routines will take over, and time will just go by. That's when we have to stop, think, and talk with each other. Lots of baggage will gather even in solid, lifelong relationships, but it's also important to have reasonable expectations for each other. "The small, everyday odds and ends are the glue that holds family life together," as His Majesty the King said rather surprisingly on his sixtieth birthday.

The best way to get a grip on the future is to try to build it yourself. Have a little planning luncheon with your wife twice a month, preferably at a lovely restaurant. Be an active, intimate discussion partner and talk about what you want to do; pencil in some activities you can do together in a pocket calendar. Only solve one big question at a time. That's more than enough.

See the strengths in your wife, not just the flaws. Perhaps she will discover the same in you, and forget all the breadcrumbs you've dropped on your shirt. For many old men, that's a hope best relegated to quiet prayers. But someone's got to start, so why not you? Pointing the finger is completely irrelevant. Just think how many crazy habits of yours your wife has had to deal with!

Forgiveness, time and time again, for all the stupid things you do is something you can get almost exclusively from your family. So start by hugging your wife, right here, right now, for at least six seconds or your serotonin levels will stay right where they are—not to mention testosterone levels!

Love is an abstract word. It's the manifestation of love that's important. My wife is both my greatest love and my best friend.

42

SUGGESTIONS FOR YOUR DAILY AGENDA

Set a goal for the coming year, and another, more general one for the following years, and take a quick look over your plans.

• Find new, fun ways to meet up with your children and grandchildren. Create new traditions and celebrations.

• Do something new and entertaining with your grandchildren. Travel with them, for example, once a year. It doesn't need to be anything expensive or lengthy. A roadtrip with Grandpa is a great adventure in its own right. It's good to create new connections and experiences they won't forget, and in turn we won't be forgotten.

• Find new, undemanding ways to socialize with friends. You don't have to serve an elaborate dinner. Gather them for tea and biscuits on Sunday. Serve beer and snacks for any everyday evening and go to the movies together.

• Having good friends at this age is at least as important as having children. We're more often on the same wavelength with our friends than with our children—since our children live in completely different worlds than we do.

• Create new interests together. It's time to fill the word "we" with new meaning. New interests lead to new connections and new friends.

• As I write this, I'm reminded that I've always wanted to go fishing. My wife is nodding in agreement. What's more, fishing is something our grandchildren may enjoy doing, and something their parents never have time for. Bingo! Gone fishing!

Give each other praise. This makes everything easier. Neither of you will be happy if the other's not satisfied in life. The goal is to change and grow together. This is when we can really live life to the fullest.

You actually can't rule out the possibility that your wife makes great sacrifices for you that you never notice; indeed, this is quite likely the case. Caring for a healthy man at home, as women jokingly say. Nothing is as hard as seeing yourself from the outside, but give it the old college try. It will only be appreciated.

Keep in mind that we can only change other people by changing ourselves.

43

WHAT KIND OF OLD MAN ARE YOU?

When my children were little, they often liked to hear what they were like as babies. Perhaps it's not such a bad idea to ask your significant other what you're like as an old man: boring? grumpy? or joyful!

But I don't think she'd appreciate you calling her a "cheery old woman." The asymmetry between men and women is, after all, significant. Perhaps that's why so many of our fellow men eavesdrop on their wives' telephone conversations. We always get to learn something new—especially about ourselves!

Keep in mind that the two of you also remember things differently. Be generous enough to each other to recognize this and take it into account. Don't lock yourself shut. Men often have a harder time giving and receiving love because they are afraid to appear weak. Be thankful for the openings you get. With my wife, I can be myself—fully.

Living together means giving and taking— the magical word: compromise. This isn't just to be fair; it's necessary.

So make sure the two of you maintain your contacts with the outside world, with friends and with society at large. It's important to stay connected and plugged in now that we've disengaged from our professional roles. Otherwise, we'll easily get disconnected.

44

DO SOMETHING UNEXPECTED!

Don't always be so predictable! Take a taxi to a hotel and check in. Lay down on the bed and take a nap. Maybe they have a pool and sauna? Order a cup of tea or a glass of champagne. Go out and eat a jolly good dinner. Sit in the bath and dream. Get in bed with a good book. Sleep well. Order breakfast in bed, along with a newspaper. Lay back, read, and relax. Eat lunch, and then take a taxi back home.

. . . But don't forget to bring your partner with you!

45

HELP YOURSELF BY HELPING OTHERS

For many of us, it's important to help others in order to give more meaning to our own lives. Here, the possibilities are nearly endless, from reading to patients in hospitals and helping children with homework to various types of mentorships. Happy is he who teaches others.

For those without a family of their own, there are many young families who would love to have an extra grandfather or grandmother to help out every once in a while. In America, there's a business that hires out older folk: Rent A Grandma. Then they can even get a grandpa as a free bonus, because it's more fun to do things together.

But for older men, there's actually a challenge that trumps all others: manhood and masculinity is, no doubt, going through changes at present. How can we help angry young men form a sound image of what it means to be a man in order to prevent much of the violence and vandalism that characterizes many modern societies?

I wish I had an answer to this question. My experience is that most of us avoid or look away from the problem in order to preserve our sanity, or to avoid feeling discouraged. But it's not sustainable if everyone does it.

46

LET YOUR INTERESTS
BECOME A NEW CAREER

A year ago, the cover of Sweden's largest financial newspaper had a large headline covering the entire first page: "The veterans' revenge."

The article was about all the people of the business world who have taken up new professional assignments in their seventies. People with experience and perspective are more desirable than ever as society is fed up with the young business tycoons who have, time and again, rocked the economic boat with their endless gambling with our assets. A few months earlier, the *Wall Street Journal* had run a similar story, but about eighty-year-olds. The Americans are always one step ahead!

This means that there is increased demand for the kind of knowledge and experience you and I have. We can apply this to tasks and mentorships within business and society. Here, too, new possibilities open up for businesses within the service sector: travel, experiences, culture, and care; after all, who better to cater to our needs than those of like mind and age?

47

DON'T MEDDLE IN OTHER PEOPLE'S BUSINESS

The older we get, the more tolerant we ought to be. It's time to stop having an opinion about what others do and how they do it. There are plenty of things I don't like in today's society. But I don't complain, because it doesn't get me anywhere. It's about time for us to put aside our pet peeves for good. Being able to crack a joke at your own expense, rather than the expense of others, is the greatest example of inner harmony.

Personally, I've grown more tolerant with the passing years. But that doesn't mean that my commitment to others has increased—quite the opposite. A healthy dose of indifference creates a peaceful foundation in interpersonal relationships. It can even be necessary.

Our time here on Earth

48

REJOICE IN YOUR
TIME ON EARTH

When my children were born, I read the
Swedish poet Erik Lindorm's fine poem "Lyckans
minut" ("Fortune's Minute") at their baptism. It
makes me happy each time I hear it and I look
forward to reading it at my grandchildren's
baptisms. That aside, Erik Lindorm is almost
forgotten today—and there is no English translation
of that poem. But a single such poem is enough to
prove that the poet did not live for naught.

I have a favorite American poem that
conveys much of the same message:

"Sing like no one is listening,
Love like you've never been hurt,
Dance like nobody is watching
And live like it's heaven on Earth."

MARK TWAIN

It's still our time here on Earth.

49

DON'T LET LIFE BECOME ONE LONG WAIT

The big pitfall in life is that all too often we wait for someone else to make the first move; we become reactive instead of active. For many of us, life becomes one long wait for school to start, for there to be a coffee break, for it to be summer, for arrival at the destination, for retirement. And then?

Don't forget that it's always your move. When it comes down to choosing between tomorrow or today, you should always choose today. Live now and die later.

"There is no meaning but that which we create ourselves."

French philosopher J. P. SARTRE

50

SAFEGUARD SUNDAYS

Modern society has made us increasingly disconnected from traditions and rituals. I think it's a very bad thing when all the days of the week become the same. This is a great risk to the young, who are always connected and available. But it's just as great a problem for us seniors, when the days feel so alike that we get them confused. We can't always drive in second gear.

I don't personally belong to any religious community, but I do believe that we've lost something essential by throwing the day of rest out along with religion. We need at least one day a week where everything else is closed, and we're open to our inner selves. When we change the tempo, and everyday routines fall away. I settle down with a poetry collection and turn on some Russian liturgical music.

Doing this is important; we give ourselves space to breathe in our everyday lives and take a break from routine—both in our heads and in our homes. We need rituals to reconcile our inner selves. The day of rest is an opportunity to let our inner voices speak and feel that we're involved in something greater. For these reasons, we should defend the silence in libraries, in churches, and in nature, giving our souls room to breathe.

51

EVEN RETIREES NEED VACATIONS

Life becomes more varied and exciting when one safeguards the summer as a time for vacation. When we're at our summer home in the country, we live differently. There, an outdoors culture, completely separate from our indoor lives at home, prevails. There, we experience the changing of the seasons in a raw, physical way. Personally, I like to put on a pair of shorts and feel like a kid again. We go for a morning dip in the ocean and read the local newspaper over breakfast in the garden. We try to do all our errands by bicycle. We push the TV from our minds and sit outside reading. We meet new people in the garden—summer friends—and look forward to impromptu visitors. We read books just for fun and always find new favorites. Every day I nap under the apple tree. And I try to refrain from working on any new projects.

It really is a completely different life, and every one of us needs it. After all, how many more times will we get to experience the budding on the rosebushes? I have perhaps ten summers left, if that. That's a frightening thought. So I really have to live those summers to their fullest.

52

STOP GRUMBLING ABOUT THE HOLIDAYS

For many, the holidays—for us Christmas—are the pinnacle of family life. Young and old alike love traditions where the whole family can gather round and do things the way we've always done them: "That's how it's always been!"

It's the young and the old who really hold Christmas—and the family—together. When our generation is gone, our children often stop celebrating Christmas together, and our grandchildren may easily lose touch with their cousins.

But we'll never get our childhood Christmases back. That's something that a lot of older folks can't get over. Today, there are far too many stepchildren and step-grandchildren, not to mention their boy- and girlfriends, step-parents, and their old mothers, sometimes with an ex-husband from an earlier marriage, for there to be complete harmony on Christmas Eve. You know exactly what I mean.

"The only true paradise is that which one has lost," to quote the French author Marcel Proust. This is both consolation and an explanation.

But Christmas continues to be a necessary break from the winter gloom, this festive time of candles and strings of blinking lights, with its traditions, food and drink, songs and midnight mass. One cannot simply throw Christmas out without becoming so much poorer.

One way to create harmony is to spread out and divide events into several installments. We usually eat well on the 23rd and decorate the tree together with some children and grandchildren. Christmas Eve morning, we serve tea with gingerbread and saffron buns, and read the gospel of Luke with a few other family members.

At our house, Christmas Eve dinner has become a big, traditional feast with as many family members as possible—but without the unwrapping of Christmas gifts, as is the Swedish custom. These are taken home by each and every one to be unwrapped later. Since we have American sons-in-law, they've started to put together a Christmas day brunch. Only then do we hand out our gifts, in full daylight and while fully conscious.

In sum, it's been a wonderful holiday—and long!

All retirees
worry about
money

53

"LET'S BE REASONABLE"

It just wouldn't do to avoid giving any advice about money in a book for happy old men, though it may stand in stark contrast to the wisdom and peace we all want to achieve. But all human activities involve economy. Life consists of matters big and small, and thoughts about money haunt many people like demons. If you have no money, you're worried about that. If you've got money, you're worried about it, too. Thus, it's important to look at money from a greater perspective and not allow financial matters to bully us.

"Let's be reasonable," as the Chinese philosopher Lin Yutang so often said. Of course, this seems to be much easier said than done. What's more, the subject of old people and money often invites jokes and ridicule. In literature, film, and theatre, retirees are often depicted as stingy, greedy people who make themselves ridiculous in various ways. Subsisting on jars of cat food is one example I remember from my childhood. Today, this is called ageism, and ought to be as taboo as making jokes about ethnicity or disabilities.

But the image of poor retirees lives on, and causes considerable stress, particularly for those who will soon be retiring. The yearly financial statements have hardly done anything to calm anyone. Despite that, I was actually taken aback when I once caught a recently retired government official in the office supply closet, filling his pockets—with paper clips!

54

WE DON'T NEED TO SCRIMP ON EVERYTHING

Today's young elderly don't need to scrimp on everything like in the olden days. Most younger seniors, between sixty-five and seventy-five years, have been the big winners in the Swedish economy since the turn of the millennium and consider their own personal economies to be good. Expenses are different and fewer as you age. According to Global Age Watch, Sweden is on top when it comes to the standards and welfare of the elderly. That's why it's gotten so much easier to become a jolly gent.

However, it's still the case that we seniors have to make sure that we can afford our everyday habits; otherwise, we have to adjust them. As a general rule: don't worry too much until you've gone over your expenses after your first full year in retirement; oftentimes, it's better than you might expect.

55

DON'T TALK ABOUT MONEY

When I was young in Sweden, people never spoke about money. But when I moved to America, it seemed that everyone talked about money, both their own and that of others. Money you had earned yourself was a source of pride, something to be shown off. Unfortunately, things have gotten to be that way here in Sweden, too.

But talking about money can never make you happy. On the contrary, chances are you'll be struck by a feeling of emptiness inside. And you may wind up saying something stupid and end up regretting it later. You'll also hear a good deal that has the potential to upset your own good humor, for jealousy is a powerful force that seems to be capable of being awakened in anyone, at any time.

But are we wiser than that? I think not.

56

AN ECONOMIC PHILOSOPHY

We all need an economic philosophy. Mine was the Crocodile Fund, something which shaped my sense of economy early on, and has followed me throughout my life. Here's how it went:

As a child, I had a model electric train. As the years went on, I built up a great big set that had just about everything, except the Crocodile, which was the top of the line in the train catalog. The Crocodile was the Swiss state railway's most powerful locomotive, jointed into three sections in order to handle the tight, narrow curves in the many Alpine tunnels. This toy model cost an unobtainable 315 kronor, a fortune at that time, certainly 8000 kronor ($1200) today.

I loved the Crocodile, I dreamt about it constantly, and I even got dizzy seeing the Swiss Alpine landscapes in which the Crocodile was at home.

One birthday, I received a white envelope with three gray 100 kronor banknotes folded in two—they were as big as napkins back then—and a blue ten and a yellow five! I was overwhelmed, never having seen that much money before.

Now I could buy the Crocodile, I thought, and hurried immediately down to the toy store, opened the glass door with the tinkling chime, and went up to the glass counter with its many treasures. There on a track stood the Crocodile with two heavy cast-iron tank cars, just waiting for me.

I finally held the coveted locomotive in my hands. I twisted and turned it about, but somehow it shrank before my eyes. I became doubtful.

Was it really worth all my fortune?
What if I were disappointed?

Wouldn't it be better to save all that money?

I took out my wallet, folding and unfolding the great bills several times. The salesman asked if he should wrap the train. I shook my head and returned my wallet to my pocket.

"I'll be back," I said, stepping quickly toward the door. But that was an absolute lie, for I knew that I was never coming back; I would never buy the Crocodile. Relieved, I ran the whole way home.

Those 315 kronor ended up in a savings account at the bank instead, which my father called the Crocodile Fund. It was great to feel so rich.

Since then, I have always been a saver, and have had very little understanding for the problems that wasters bring unto themselves. If more people thought that way, we wouldn't have just been standing in the middle of the greatest debt crisis in the history of man.

"As you make your bed, so must you lie upon it," as the proverb goes.

57

IT'S TIME TO LEAVE THE STOCK MARKET

The '40s kids have long had legendary great luck. But all of Europe and the United States have found itself in a deep debt crisis for the last few years, and most things are now depreciating in value.

For many, stock trading became something of a sport in the 1980s. But things are different now, and stocks have once again become the high-risk speculation they really always were. One day they go up, and the next they go down, and many follow the exchange with their hearts in their throats. The time of two-figure yields has come and most definitely gone.

It's time for us to leave the stock market. Our need for adventurous investments decreases over the years.

58

YOU ONLY NEED TWO PIECES OF ADVICE

The best investment is to pay off your remaining debts. As a senior, it's most pressing to bring down current expenses so they are as low as possible. Don't ever mortgage your house again. So-called senior loans on your house only mean that you risk being stuck without a roof over your head when you decide in your eighties that you want to move—we '40s kids will end up living longer than we expect, so look out!

The next best investment is to place your savings in continuous three-month investment accounts at the bank. This forces you to think before incurring large expenses. You'll become less prone to those big, unnecessary purchases. It's really worth it, trust me!

59

SING AS YOU PAY YOUR BILLS

Here's what I do to make the chore of paying bills go by as quickly as possible, and prevent it from interrupting the joys of life:

Once a month, I take out the bills, pour a drink, turn on a CD with some old favorites, and then begin filling out the paperwork. It's actually kind of cozy, the evening doesn't end up wasted, and all the paid bills go neatly into a folder. In this way, paying bills becomes a rather pleasant evening of music, and I remain a happy old man.

60

ONLINE BANKING?
THERE IS A TIME AND PLACE
FOR EVERYTHING

It's much more difficult to enjoy online banking, which requires that I concentrate, refrain from drinking, and turn off the music to concentrate. When you get older, it's hard to see the small digits on the screen. Bifocals only seem to make matters worse in front of the screen.

This usually ends up with me hunched forward without glasses, head on the screen and bills under my nose. No, that's no cozy evening, I guarantee you that.

When the banks wonder why so many of us stubbornly continue on with checks and paper statements, well, perhaps they'll find part of their answer here.

61

WE ALL HAVE TWO CAREERS— ONE AT WORK, AND ONE AT THE BANK

For most of us, "career" is a word that has to do with how successful we are in our work. But there are many for whom a fat bank account is a sign of how successful we are in life.

The best one can say about money is that money gives us freedom. Though "much would have more" comes as the usual result, and just like that, all the gains are lost.

Most of us have met successful people who have downright failed in their personal finances. It's more common than you'd think. Equally

common are people who have earned quite
a bit of money without winning the respect of
society. This is neither fair nor unfair, but simply
two different ways of relating to life.

62

ALWAYS LIVE BELOW YOUR MEANS

We like to compare ourselves to others, but appearances are so very deceptive. Many houses are mortgaged right up to the chimney, and others are completely loan-free. Some people have leased cars. Others own theirs. Our car is seventeen years old. All my tweed jackets are ancient, but comfortable. Today this is called vintage, and it's very much in style, so be thankful.

A good tip has always been to live below your means: underspend. I've always done it. This creates both economic buffers and calm in your soul.

But one thing is clear: if everyone lived this way, our society would end up in an eternal recession. That's the paradox of modern civilization.

63

LOOK OUT FOR PROPERTY-ANXIETY DISORDER

Many '40s kids have gathered houses, vacation homes, and places to stay in the mountains or in other countries. The risk that comes with all these properties is that there are constantly new questions coming up about maintenance, upkeep, repairs, taxes, and other expensive things. This gradually results in the development of property-anxiety disorder, which has the following symptoms:

1. Repairs are never done on time.
2. More and more vacations are spent at construction sites.

3. Your bags fill up with construction dust.
4. Every trip unleashes new practical problems.
5. Windowed envelopes containing bills are stacked up high.
6. Everything ends up being more expensive than you thought—in other words, much ado about nothing.
7. You become anxious and can't sleep because of all these practicalities.

If this is the case, it's about time for you get rid of your property anxiety.

64

DO NOT BORROW OR LEND ANYTHING

There are good reasons for us older people to be careful with our money. One who is in debt is not free. Most of us can't generate additional income anymore. We have what we have, and it's got to last us the rest of our lives. There's a big difference between being wise and being stingy.

Don't lend money to others, either; then they'll be in your debt. It can be uncomfortable for both of you, and such debts have ruined many a friendship. It's actually almost as uncomfortable to be a creditor as it is to be a debtor.

"One who lends to a friend gets himself an enemy," as the old proverb says.

65

BEWARE OF YOUR CHILDREN'S DEALINGS

We've reached the age where we know ourselves pretty well and can make relatively wise decisions. We know what makes us feel good and what stresses us out. So don't let anybody—especially not your children—drag you into complicated affairs, sureties, or investments that disturb your peace of mind or force you to take out loans. What's more, this will poison your relationship with your children. A loan quickly becomes a wound that never heals.

What matters, then, is to dare to say no. It's not self-interest, but a way to take care of your health, both physically and mentally. Stress in old age quickly leads to worry and confusion that can trigger dementia.

66

PRIDE COMES BEFORE
A FALL

It sounds rather old-fashioned, but there's no
doubt that there are eternal truths contained in
this old proverb. The ancient Greeks knew that
nothing was more dangerous than pride—or
hubris, as they called it—for then, the gods
would have their revenge.

In our time, too, the nouveau riche commonly
appear to be seized with pride, only to lose all
their money. Divine justice, it's called, as they
bring themselves down.

We all know that money is necessary to live
a good life, but it isn't all that's needed. "Not by
bread alone," as it says in the Bible, though we

seem to have forgotten that. Perhaps it's because today, we're stricken by one financial crisis after another? Perhaps this is the gods' revenge?

After the Biblical seven years of abundance come the seven years of famine. Nothing is new under the sun.

67

USE WHAT YOU
ALREADY HAVE

Advertising agencies call us WOOPs—
well-off older people—and are trying to figure
out how they can reach us with their marketing.
But we seniors are individuals, and don't want
to be treated as a group. We Baby Boomers
follow no predictable trends, instead we will
transform our lives in old age, just as we did
when we were young. I myself will use what
I already have at hand. Besides, all the new
things at the mall look alike.

What's more, the difference between dreams
and reality has never been as great as when it
comes to today's gadgets. As soon as you get

home, you can see the cracks and scratches. In many cases, items fall apart after the first week. Most of it is rubbish, but then again, it is manufactured in countries with dismal wages, so what do you expect?

68

INVEST IN THINGS THAT DON'T COST

During my life, I've lived in several parts of the world. In the summers, we've sailed many waters around the Baltic Sea—Swedish, Finnish, Estonian, and Latvian—and around Long Island in America. Every time, I bring back a beautiful stone typical of the region. I've put these stones in a sort of little cobblestone terrace in my garden in southern Sweden. While I drink my tea in my deck chair, I can take a short trip in my mind to the many places I've gotten to visit in the world. It costs nothing.

69

THE BABY BOOMERS ARE CHECKING OUT

Sweden's largest and richest generation is in the process of moving from grand villas and apartments to smaller residences. This means we've got to get rid of tons of stuff. This is a completely natural demographic process. The problem becomes that there are fewer and fewer buyers for our things, and so the prices sink.

But it's not just about fewer young people with purchasing power. There's also the increased tendency to move from place to place and new values. The younger generation doesn't want to lug around all the baggage we've created. They don't want to polish silver, copper, or bronze. They'd also rather not maintain all the items and properties we have. Why buy a cabin in the mountains if you're only there for two weeks out of the year? The younger generation wants to live a richer, more mobile lifestyle rather than tying up its money. It's a question of lifestyle. In that respect, they're doing things completely right.

70

HELP! THE CHILDREN DON'T WANT OUR ANTIQUES EITHER!

Several of us have noticed that our children would rather not have our antiques. "Twelve dining room chairs? No thanks, but we can take two of them for the hall."

This creates a good deal of stress among many seniors who thought that their homes represented great assets for their children to take over later. We've gotten used to the idea of everything going up in value: art, antiques, boats, stamps, coins, collectible plates, and so on. People hoard like squirrels and most of it seemed to have been a good investment—until now.

Many today are worried and are unwilling to sell their assets at the plummeting prices. Personally, I think you ought to sell only to get rid of things, and to at least get a bit of money for them, and to avoid continued stress. No thief can take from us the essentials of life: our knowledge, experiences, and memories—none save for doctor Alzheimer himself, and death, of course.

71

ENJOY LIFE INSTEAD

When we become seniors, we suddenly have a lot more time. We ought to enjoy it. Continuing to contemplate money and its worth can easily upset the rest of our lives. We recall how rich Uncle Scrooge McDuck was, how he dove into his money, but we forget how alarmed he always was at the thought of someone taking it. This was precisely the point of the whole comic book series.

So let's be more like Gladstone Gander and enjoy life instead. After all, shrouds don't have pockets and we have no use for those extra bucks once we're gone.

The riddles
of time

72

NOT ALL TIME IS CREATED EQUAL

"More happens in London in a day than in India in a whole lifetime," Gandhi wrote after visiting England in 1913.

We ought to be thankful for time, so that we can do one thing at a time. Otherwise, everything would happen all at once, all the time, according to physicists. That would really be stressful. As it is, there will, thankfully, always be tomorrow.

Not all time is created equal. Even the pharaohs of Egypt knew this. Some generations live during good times, others during bad ones.

Some generations are lucky; others are not, and they end up right in the middle of wars and depressions. After the good years come the bad ones—and vice versa, thank goodness. As proof: the Swedes of the 1940s have had historical luck. Times were good, and so were we.

Time does not treat all people and cultures equally. Some have had great booms they look back to, in places like Athens, Rome, and Paris. Others are young and hungry, and they look to the future, as is the case with many Asian countries today. China has seen many great cultures and slumps during its 3000+ years. The Roman Empire's collapse and fall has unsettled people in the West since the Renaissance. Can it happen again? What were the reasons it failed? Historians usually point to two factors—increased migration patterns and a new fanatical religion: Christianity. Does it sound familiar? Well, that is precisely the question.

Sweden as a kingdom has a nearly one-thousand-year-old history. Where we're headed today, no one knows. He who lives shall see. But the starting point ought to be that our best time is now.

> "History never repeats itself, but it rhymes every once in a while."
>
> MARK TWAIN

The older I get, the better are the books I want to read. It's no longer worth wasting time on the bad ones. I'd rather read classics that have withstood the test of time for decades—not to mention centuries—than all the thrillers or crime novels that will fall by the wayside. So much for Swedish noir.

It's not a bad idea to get help from those who came before us. Holding a dialogue with a person who lived several hundred years ago—perhaps even thousands of years ago—is both wise and instructive, and gives us a sense of perspective and meaning. Like the Italian Renaissance poet Dante, we're not without guides on our journey. Each and every one of us has his own Virgil.

73

TO BE A PART OF
SOMETHING GREATER

At one point in time, people understood
themselves as parts of a greater whole: a
family, a farm, a clan, a nation, or a religion.
Back then, it was easy to see yourself as a link
in a greater sort of food chain, and earlier
generations were spiritually present among the
living ones.

Our modern focus on the individual makes
it so that we can find little comfort in this. Our
engaged perspective often stretches no further
than to children and grandchildren. With great-
grandchildren, we've gone too far for most people.

"It gets too diluted," as a ninety-year-old said to me. I'd sooner think that we should see generations like chain letters or Matryoshka dolls: it's important not to break the link.

People who belong to families with a history, a business, or a family estate often take solace in this sense of belonging. The family becomes something greater than the individual people themselves, and the family's development over generations becomes a source of support for the individual.

74

EITHER-OR

I have always been fascinated by the hyphen in either-or. Here there exists a concentration of time, gathered together. It's like a skate jump. You begin with a motion in one direction—and come down in the other. It's almost like flying over the International Date Line.

The Danish philosopher Kirkegaard called his only novel *Either/Or*. It's about two different approaches to life, the ethic and the aesthetic. The greater part of our contemporaries have chosen Or—the aesthetic approach, enjoyment. But if we can't determine right from wrong and take responsibility for our choices, things won't go too well for us.

Nothing brings time to a head like an airport; after all, it's only there to be passed through. It either goes smoothly and quickly, or we're soon bogged down in a thick syrup of delays and cancelled flights.

"Time is like eternity folded into an accordion," to quote the French film editor Jean Cocteau.

The moment that just passed was, after all, recently "now."

When I was young, a family dinner and an evening with friends would often collide. You either did what your parents wanted—or you ventured out with your friends. In both cases, either something had to be sacrificed or a conflict had to be dealt with. Today, young folks meet so late in the evening that they actually make it to family dinners, and then go out with friends afterward. Not everything was better before.

There's no such thing as immortality

75

FAME IS THE SUN
OF THE DEAD

Andy Warhol had described modern fame already when we were young: "In the year 2000, everybody will be famous for fifteen minutes."

At that time, the year 2000 seemed tremendously distant, and Warhol's prediction seemed very profound. But now we've passed this milestone, too, without anything exceptional happening. Perhaps we will live in virtual immortality on Facebook, floating in a digital cloud without beginning and without end— because who really has all the passwords to our digital identities? Perhaps we ought to include them in our wills?

On the other hand, Warhol was right in his own way. Just look at all the winners of "Survivor" flashing by on television, only to end up in media-oblivion for the rest of their lives. Perhaps only in obituaries, if even then, will their few seconds of fame flash before us once again. It's no wonder so many young people develop psychological issues. Life seems to be over before it's really even begun.

Thoughts of immortality fall flat on their faces. "In the long run, we're all dead," as the British economist Lord Keynes expressed the matter when faced with the advantages of long-term investment decision. I have a hard time understanding why our souls are supposedly so interesting. It seems absurd that we would all gain eternal life somewhere. Heaven would be a pretty crowded place.

That aside, we can probably hope to live on in our children's and grandchildren's lives. We exist as long as they remember. So invite them to a fun weekend now!

76

THE QUESTION OF LIFE AND DEATH CHARACTERIZES ALL GREAT ART

All artists hope for immortality, but it is bestowed upon only a few.

"Come and visit me in a thousand years!" bellowed the Russian poet Mayakovsky across the grand arenas in the 1920s, shaking his fist at the sky.

A brilliant artist who dies early seems to have a better chance at immortality than an artist who lives a long life. As I write this, I've just read this headline: "Death made Sylvia Plath immortal." Over the young, dead author lingers a sense of romance that disappears from the old, decrepit ones. Sorry about that.

So by now we're probably too old to be immortal!

77

EVERYONE WANTS TO BE SEEN

Hjalmar Söderberg writes in *Doctor Glas*: "One wants to be loved; or, failing that, feared; or, failing that, despised and scorned. One would like to inspire some sort of feeling in other people. The soul shudders before the void, and wants contact, no matter the price."

Söderberg's description explains a lot of the bitterness around us. People want to be recognized, but it doesn't happen. That makes them unhappy and disgruntled. We often meet them on the Internet today. Hatred toward authority and superiority wells up everywhere. Ordinary people strike back against the media's echo chambers. The Internet is free and dangerous. It's not much of a place for happy old men to hang around, unless we want to become less happy.

I think I prefer the French author André Malraux's view: "The only thing one owns in another man is that which he changes in him."

That's an attractive thought.

78

BE HAPPY FOR WHAT YOU'VE GOTTEN

When I was visiting the Gothenburg Book Fair, I found myself next to a used book seller. Curious as I was, I asked him how my children's books were doing on the second-hand book market.

"We never get them in," he replied. When he saw how baffled I was, he explained: "The reason is that parents rarely get rid of historic children's books when their kids have grown up. Instead, they move the books out to their vacation homes and put them on their bookshelves on the verandah, where they stand and wait for the next generation." I was quite pleased with that answer, not to mention beaming.

79

EACH AND EVERY ONE OF US TINKERS WITH HIS OWN MUSEUM

For quite some time now, I've been in the habit of tucking cards and photographs into the books I read and then replacing them on my shelves. This has made it so that, time and again, I get unexpected greetings from the person I once was, and the life I lived at the time.

In our summer home, drawings and photographs of the older generation hang on the walls. For the coming grandchildren, I hide old coins and other small things in boxes and bowls. One day they'll come and find them, twisting and turning them and thinking about what the world was like back then. But by then we will most likely find ourselves in Her Majesty Queen Victoria's of Sweden tenth year regnant. That is also why the old black and white photo of King Gustav VI Adolf will hang on under the attic stairs. Was it so long ago? The foremost role of a monarchy in a rapidly changing world is to measure time and divide it into epochs. Victorian, anyone?

In the kitchen, there's a thriving *Gynostemma pentaphyllum*, the herb of immortality. Once in a while I add a few leaves of it to my tea and continue building my sandcastles.

80

WE'LL NEVER QUITE BE COMPLETELY DEAD

The Swedish artist Einar Hylander was out walking High Street one dark autumn evening. A first-floor window was open. He paused when he saw one of his paintings filling an entire wall, and stopped, fascinated, to look. As old as he was, he was delighted to see that his art would make people happy long after he himself had died.

Suddenly, a young woman appeared in the window, stared at him, and slammed the window shut, cutting her off as she yelled to someone in the back of the room: "There's an old creep staring . . ." Einar smiled to himself and went on walking. Such are the terms of being an artist.

"Non omnis moriar"—I shall never die completely—has been the solace of artists and authors throughout the centuries.

Even the female Greek poet Sappho (600s BC) realized the great capacity of the written arts to travel through time: "Someone, I say, will remember us henceforth." Prove her right, and borrow her poems from the library now!

81

NOSTALGIA IS THE LEADING NARCOTIC AMONG THE ELDERLY

Occasionally, I'll venture into the sphere of the Church, which is a generous place and always open. You can participate, even if you doubt. The church year itself is a comforting tour through time that repeats every year, even for the skeptic; traditions and holidays come at set times and there is comfort in this familiar cycle for us older folk.

For the eternal child inside me, the old psalms play a particularly emotional role. I can easily burst out in tears on hearing the notes of *Den blomstertid nu kommer* (Now the Time of

Blossoming Arrives). It's the most Swedish hymn you can find, in its ingenious interweaving of nature and religious themes.

Härlig är jorden (Lovely Is the Earth) is another one I can't make it through without a lump forming in my throat. Particularly gripping is the phrase "släkten följa släktens gång . . ." (each generation follows the path of the previous) which really gives you a strong sense of your place in the natural order. Everything feels so much lighter.

82

WE WANT RETIREMENT HOMES WITH SINGING AND DANCING

For those of us who once entrusted our parents to a long-term care facility, we were simply left without a choice. Who can forget how all the staff just sat in the break room and smoked? And when we voiced our opinion about the care they gave, they usually took it badly and called the union.

No, there really were no guarantees. It was not better before.

The Baby Boomers do not want to be humiliated like that. We don't want to live where the staff work; we want their services in our own homes. Their rules about work environments can't be allowed to threaten our integrity. If we want a pet dog or cat, it shouldn't be our problem if one of the staff members is allergic. We don't want to watch aquarium fish swimming around on a TV screen for hours. No, we want to play video games like Grand Theft Auto V instead!

We '40s kids were the first teenagers, and we're used to being the ones calling the shots. Rock 'n' roll gave us a vitality and empowerment that sets us apart from earlier generations. But now we've moved on. We're not going to be content and thankful for the obvious. We want to have our interests and particular needs fulfilled. We don't all want to knit or whittle, the only allowed interests in old folks' homes. No, we want to be wine tasting retirees and stoner pensioners, so look out!

The politicians warn us that society won't have enough resources. But society spends up to ten times more caring for a prisoner than for a pensioner. A career criminal costs society 80 million kronor ($12.5 million) during his life. Who makes these decisions? We ought to ask that question the next time someone claims that retirees cost too much.

83

IT'S NOT TOO EASY TO BEAT AN OLD-TIMER

Most of us have realized that we have a long time left, and that life is full of opportunities. The entertainment industry has realized that too, so now there's a Swedish TV show called *Can You Beat an Old-Timer?* On this show, thirty- to forty-year-old couch potatoes compete in physical challenges against Iron Grandmas and Grandpas in their seventies and eighties.

Naturally, there was discussion in the media about whether or not the show was offensive to the young fatties. That's what some experts thought, but none of the fatties agreed. On the contrary, they found it stimulating to see healthy, vigorous old-timers and saw them as good examples.

So stand up straight! It's fun to be a model of old age.

Death, and other odds and ends

84

FACE TO FACE WITH DEATH

Seldom do we come face to face with death. As a young man, living was the obvious thing to do; I didn't think for a second about death. For me, it wasn't until I was thirty-eight, when my father died, that I first contemplated dying. My father had Alzheimer's disease, so I ought to have been prepared when death struck, but I wasn't.

Confucius, the Chinese statesman and philosopher who lived in the 500s BC, expressed this matter as follows:

"How can one understand death before he understands life?"

A great divide runs between life and death. And the border between life and death is but a single breath. For this reason, we are never fully prepared. But when the breaths ceased, I was suddenly alone in the hospital room, and my father no longer existed. His soul had left his body and left the room; a candle had been blown out. You could almost grasp the emptiness.

It is often said that when an old person dies, a whole library burns up. We're never quite as overwhelmed as we are when death strikes. Death is the only thing that can derail modern man's electronic calendars and schedules. Suddenly, there is no longer any freedom of choice.

But when a person dies, the world doesn't even hiccup. We stand there, paralyzed—and everything continues on as usual around us. The parking lot guard makes his rounds outside the hospital window where my father lies, and I grow anxious.

Truthfully, life is made up of things both big and small. The old die, and children continue to be born. As it should be.

85

NOTHING IS QUITE SO
BANAL AS DEATH

We are headed toward death wherever we go. We have lived, we have done our part, whatever it may have been. It is from earth that we have come, and it is earth that we shall become once more. Our medieval churches depict the so-called Wheel of Life in powerful frescos. First, there is the young person on his way up the wheel; then, he rides victoriously on his success; but after comes the inevitable fall; and finally, death stands waiting with his scythe.

Even the biblical King David had a ring with the inscription: "This too shall pass." The ring is a symbol of eternity. It has neither beginning nor end.

We all live in death's waiting room. It is nonetheless somewhat comforting that we aren't waiting alone. At the same time, death is the most individual experience imaginable; as each and every one of us must walk through the exit completely alone. But for some of us, death is also an entrance, to finally come home or meet those who are near and dear, but who died before us; till death do us reunite.

My death is mine, even if Freud considers that "deep down, nobody believes in their own death." I admit, I probably don't. "The churchyard is peaceful, but few wish to go there," says the old proverb.

My grandchild says to me:

"Spiders are worse than death."

86

NOT EVERYBODY CAN STAND TO LOOK TRUTH IN THE EYE

"Almost all of us shall die," Ludvig XIV's court chaplain was forced to correct himself upon seeing how distraught the king was at the thought that he, too, would one day die.

But we know better than that. "We will all wander the path, if we live and are in good health," as was once said out in the country.

Indeed, if it's not one, it's the other.

Those of us who grew up under the Cold War's nuclear umbrella always had a gnawing, uncomfortable feeling that everything could spin out of control at any moment, that we could all die in one fell swoop. We've barely had enough time to exhale since then. And now Russia is at it again, with a president out of the Hells Angels.

In today's society, we often meet death as entertainment: in media, in mysteries, in film, and in video games. It's usually sudden, vicious death we're talking about, far from our own cozy reality. The ones dying are usually complete strangers, and rather unsympathetic villains. So let them have it!

87

LIFE IS WASTED WHEN WE BUSY OURSELVES WITH DEATH

"Hodie mihi, cras tibi"—today me; tomorrow you, as it's written in Latin on many old graves.

"Vanitas vanitatum!"—The vanity of all vanities!—echoes throughout Christian history.

But life is wasted when we busy ourselves with death. The best conclusion we can make is to use our time well. The more one has lived, the less frightening it is, actually.

"One must live such that one becomes friends with death, I think, tra la la la," as Astrid Lindgren, the author of *Pippi Longstocking*, would say in her twilight.

We've got a while left in the sailboat before we go shooting down the bays in the world's most beautiful archipelago, our backs to the sun. I take a deep breath and listen to the wind. Each time may be the last. This is how I want to spend the last day of my life.

88

WE'VE ALMOST MADE IT ALL THE WAY

We Baby Boomers have lived relatively good lives and gotten to be so old that we ought to feel more satisfaction and worry less about death. After all, we've made it almost all the way, and attained many of our goals.

But we have another problem: we all want to be so free that nobody wants to be conventional. But how can we look upon death without prejudice? Indeed, what can we expect from death?

"Oh, just ignore it," says my grandchild. Maybe I'll take her up on it.

"A world which is not this world," wrote the Polish Nobel Prize–winner Wisława Szymborska in her final collection of poems.

One of the pros of death is that most people speak well of the dead, while slander dances in circles around the living. Besides, the dead don't need to fear death any longer.

Always something.

Personally, I was most afraid of death when the children were little. But now they both have good lives with families of their own. Now, I'm finally too old to die young.

Here are the last words of the French author Rabelais, on his deathbed in 1553: "I am going to seek a great perhaps." Or as the grandchild says to me: "Isn't death the ultimate experience?"

89

YOU'VE GOT TO HAVE LUCK ALSO WITH DEATH

Health care and death overlap in our society, one which has turned death into a disease and medical specialty: geriatric and palliative care. And so we complain a lot about the care, in order to tamp down the thoughts of death. But neither society nor the nursing care staff can engage on a personal level with each and every person. Only you can warm your mother's cold hand.

Many relatives complain that the care is unfair. It certainly can be. Happy old men get better care. It's as easy as that. Care staff are people too, and they like positive old folks who entertain them to the best of their abilities. My mother was always good at getting stressed-out staff members at the nursing home where she spent her last years to laugh. They liked to come see her. It's not fair, but it's human.

90

IT'S IMPORTANT TO MAINTAIN BOTH HUMOR AND DIGNITY UNTIL THE END

We're so used to thinking in terms of choices, but there are no choices at all when it comes to death. We're done. Period. This realization can even be nice, since then we don't have to waste any more energy on it. At any rate, it doesn't matter one bit what we think, so we may as well take it easy and joke about it.

"It's not that I'm afraid to die. I just don't want to be there when it happens."

WOODY ALLEN

We must all do our utmost to die with dignity, particularly for the sake of our children. Remember that this is the last thing they'll remember about us for the rest of their lives. This will become the image that lingers with them, so let's make the best of what we can. It's never too late to show some uprightness. It's just as well to practice next time you go to the emergency room, too.

Personally, I'd like to check out before divorces, serious illnesses, and other unfortunate events strike my children. The older our children get, the more powerless we become. On such nights, the stars look coldly down at us. We're all children of decay, just passing through this life.

91

IN THE END, EVERYBODY DIES

We have to let go of everything we've collected during the course of a long life. This makes many people anxious. I personally find the fact that everyone who lived before us has died to be a comforting thought.

When even Jesus, God's own son, says on the cross "My God, why have you forsaken me?", you and I really have no reason to complain. If everybody dies, there's no need for us to feel singled out or smote down.

Quite simply, death is a part of life, of the whole bargain. It's what rounds us off. Only with death as punctuation do we know if someone has lived a good life—the whole way through.

After we die, everything we are will dissolve and merge once more with nature. We all breathe the same air breathed by all those who came before us. As a part of nature, our participation in it is greater than we usually think. I find both comfort and joy in that thought.

92

WHAT DO THE DYING COMPLAIN ABOUT MOST?

Various studies have concluded that people on their deathbeds most often regret the following things:

"Why did I spend so much time at the office? What was all of that really for?" This is the most common complaint among dying men.

"Why didn't I live like I wanted to? Why did I let other people control me so much?" This is the most common complaint among dying women.

Additionally:

"Why didn't I ever say what I really thought? Not even my own family knows who I am."

"Why did I lose so many of my friends? The smallest things often got between us."

"Why didn't I enjoy more of my life: my family, my friends, my money?"

"May I not have lived in vain," uttered Danish astronomer Tycho Brahe on his deathbed. Thankfully, that is not a question we need to answer ourselves.

93

PERHAPS DEATH WILL SOLVE THE POPULATION EXPLOSION IN ITS OWN WAY

Today, there are roughly seven billion people on Earth. That is far too many, and the pressure on the environment is increasing in an unsustainable manner. People pounce on the world's resources and pillage everything in the way. It goes quickly. Every week, the Chinese start a new coal power plant—despite knowing better. There's no doubt they're going to choke themselves—and the rest of us. In our lifetime alone, more than fifty thousand species of plants and animals have gone extinct.

Nature responds with floods, epidemics, and other catastrophes, each one worse than the last.

If we don't manage to set overpopulation straight, death will do the job for us, and humans may very well die out. Talk about the most forbidden! From this perspective, it's really not a disadvantage to have already lived the greater part of one's life.

Planting forests in Africa and Asia are vital projects for all who will continue to live here on Earth. It's the least we can do while we're still here. We no longer share a future, but we can still share the present.

94

YOU'LL TIRE OF THINKING ABOUT DEATH

As a ninety-year-old recently told me: "Every morning when I wake up, I'm always just as surprised that I'm still here."

When we reach a certain age, what we're counting is not years but hours and days. What you do doesn't need to be extraordinary. But the ability to enjoy it is. It comes down to not giving up until it's really over. Besides, when there's such little time left, it's just not right to spend it being bored!

When you get to be really old, your age in and of itself becomes a source of pride. My first father-in-law lived to be ninety years old, and was very entertaining right up to the end. He'd always put on a bit of a show when someone else from his generation was brought up in discussion: "Is he still alive?" he'd ask with mock amazement.

It's the old game of King of the Hill at play again.

"Was I there?" he might ask when we spoke of a pleasant dinner. And when we answered in the affirmative, he'd ask: "Did I have fun?" We'd all laugh, and he would be satisfied.

He was a happy old man. He enjoyed his age immensely and made the most of it.

95

DEATH IN THE POT

The question of death won't leave us alone. We forget it now and then, but we're constantly reminded of it. The older we get, the more often it comes up.

The first time I met death was . . . in a pot! I was three or four years old when mom suddenly shouted: "There's death in the pot!"

Mom had many such expressions which I figured were just part of her southern dialect, but which were actually from the Bible—in this case the second Book of Kings. What she meant, I didn't understand, but I saw death before me in a pot in our kitchen in Uppsala.

The first time I actually thought about death, I was a good nine years old or so. My father told me one day how he nearly "drove himself to death." His car had gone into a skid in the middle of a curve, when along came a large truck. He skidded onto the wrong side of the road and the truck thundered past, brakes screeching and horns honking.

"Did you think about death then?" I asked.

"No, my only thought was: why did I quit smoking?" he answered.

The answer baffled me then, just as it does today. The big thoughts don't come automatically in big moments—quite the opposite.

96

"LOVE LIFE MORE THAN ITS MEANING"

These words are Russian author Fyodor Dostoyevsky's, and this is what his writing is all about. Life isn't just about a number of years, but what you get out of them and what you can pass on to others. Life is not only a question of external success, but also *joie de vivre* and a sense of community. So you should love the life you've lived, and the day as it is.

The grace of being the subject of others' solicitude comes about most often within a family. This is precisely why we must safeguard our families.

The good life leads to something so unusual and un-modern as contentment. One finally becomes satisfied. To wander at your own pace, hands behind your back; to sit with a faraway gaze, a smile on your lips; to make contact with your innermost springs—and to sit yourself down at the regulars' table, as the Mediterranean people might add.

97

HE WHO DIES GETS TO SEE

There are a good many so-called near-death experiences people have reported. The Swedish author Artur Lundkvist lay in a coma for two months after a stroke, woke up, and was able to retell his impressions in a literary form, in the book *Journeys in Dream and Imagination*. He begins his description thus: "I know that I'm traveling the whole time, presumably without interruptions, but without any shaking and noise, silently soft . . . this must be a dream trip I'm on, an absolute dream trip, where everything is real, but everything comes to me without my even needing to wish it."

Another remarkable description comes from the Swedish journalist Göran Skytte, who in the spring of 2012 suffered a bad stroke: "During those hours in which I successively began to understand that my life was in danger, I felt no worry, no fear . . . I was afraid of neither life nor death. Instead, I felt a great calm, an inner peace. I saw not dark, but light. Those who were around me at the time say that I radiated stillness."

These experiences have made me doubtful of the new term of death, that is, brain-dead and equal to deceased though the heart still beats. What reactions in the brain might a knife stabbing into the still-living body obtain? The soul is invisible and captured inside the body's physical form. These are very difficult questions and this newfound doubt has led me to decide against being an organ donor.

98

PERHAPS THERE IS A LIGHT AT THE END OF THE TUNNEL

Swedish Nobel Prize–winner Arvid Carlsson has described in a radio program the latest findings from clinical research, which show that a cascade of electric activity occurs in the nerve cells of the brain for about half a minute after the heart stops. Carlsson thinks that this creates a final, serene experience of light and limitlessness, perhaps of the infinite. Perhaps Paradise?

When I heard him say this, I had an intense experience of happiness and thought back to Skorpan's death in Astrid Lindgren's *The Brothers*

Lionheart: "Yes, Jonathan, yes, I see the light! I see the light!"

This confirms that something really does happen in the instant of death, which those around the dying person often interpret as the soul leaving the body. Perhaps life appears then for the dying person as an instant of brilliant lucidity, merging into the infinite—from which we once came. One can only hope.

Steve Jobs's last words on his deathbed were: "Oh, wow! Oh, wow! Oh, wow!"

99

WE'LL NEVER GET OUT OF HERE WITHOUT DEATH

Time flows like a river toward death. Without a sense of time, our lives would lose their dynamism. Everything would continue on forever, and there wouldn't be a single emergency exit we could escape through.

Immortality gives me a feeling of claustrophobia. How are we supposed to get out of here then? We'd be forced to get along with our stepmothers and the same coworkers for the rest of our lives!

Time is the gust of wind that causes life's leaves to rustle; it comes from without into our lives and measures out our lifespans. Time is the creator of both tragedy and death, creation and life. It constantly blows lightly upon our necks. And suddenly, night falls.

100

BUT DON'T FORGET YOUR LAST WISH

"When God comes with death, the devil steps in with the heirs," says an old Swedish proverb. As with all proverbs, it summarizes ancient experience.

The many divorces we Baby Boomers have gone through have resulted in a new problem: stepchildren and half-siblings. Newspapers have begun to feature far too many advertisements from law firms and tax consultants with horror stories of widows and widowers who lose house and home when children from earlier marriages suddenly come knocking on the door.

The problem isn't really the stepchildren themselves. The problem is that so few of us write wills or divide up our property so that all the surviving relatives know what applies on the day we pass away. I know, because I too have been a stepchild.

The subject is, at any rate, both painful and embarrassing, and most of us put it off until the very end. Another reason is that people in normal financial circumstances never think of the will as a part of our own reality, dismissing it as a thing reserved for those with large assets to divide.

When I've finished writing this, I too will finally put together a will.

Summa
summarum

101

THERE ARE GOOD REASONS TO GO TO FUNERALS

I used to go to funerals only reluctantly. Today, I think there are numerous reasons to go. On one hand, it is important to honor old friends and acquaintances one last time. That is, after all, what funerals are all about. Joy and sorrow follow one another through life, so let us, too, follow each other.

Apart from that, funerals are the last type of social event we old folks get invited to. They give us a chance to meet people we've lost touch with during the course of life. It can be a pleasant, rewarding reunion.

When the crowd around us begins to shrink, it can be a great time to stock up on rediscovered friends. Just recently we found ourselves in the middle of a large circle of friends; now our social circle is beginning to thin out.

102

FUNERALS CAN STRENGTHEN OUR SENSE OF LIFE

My wife is part of a big, lively family. A few years ago, a death in the family brought with it a strong, shared wish to reconnect. So they arranged a big family reunion with nearly one hundred participants; it was incredibly successful. For my children, it was a good experience, as it turned out that they were second cousins to several young people they knew from school and university.

"Are we really related?"

Funerals invite us, then, to a sort of fellowship that can strengthen our sense of life. They also make it possible for you to imagine yourself as dead and mourned by those near and dear to you. Unexpected emotions get an opportunity to come forward. Besides, crying openly and freely is allowed at funerals. And a good cry is sometimes exactly what we need.

103

WE ARE NOT RESPONSIBLE FOR ARRANGING OUR OWN FUNERALS

Many worry about their own funerals, and wonder how they can make sure they go the way they want. In a certain sense, your funeral is the last event in life where you are the host.

The truth, though, is that you neither can nor should influence your own funeral except in a limited way, first by talking with your children, and second by leaving a will. It's the responsibility of those who survive us to arrange our funerals, and they may have their own ideas as well, which are just as important. It is they, after all, who will live on with the grave and the memory. The advantage of being dead is that you avoid thorny questions, after all.

You should leave the funeral arrangements to your relatives with confidence and trust.

104

WHERE DO YOU WANT TO REST?

Choosing a place to be buried can be difficult with today's broken family structures. Where should an old father lie? With his third and last wife, or with his first, with whom he had all of his children? The widow usually has one idea, the children another. The only thing anybody can agree on is that wife number two was a real bitch.

And which newspaper should the obituary be in? It seems that the people who die in *The New York Times* and the *New York Post* are completely different. In any case, no color photographs, please! We dead people look best with subdued lighting.

Many Swedes have family graves in long-lost areas in the country. This can cause problems for surviving relatives, who have no connection to this place. For these reasons, I let my children decide where their grandmother was to be buried, so that they themselves wouldn't lose track of her. I moved my great-grandparents' graves there later, so now they're all together in one place that my children have a living connection to. Perhaps they'll bury us there some day, but that's a question I won't bring up. A lot can happen. But I'm happy that I made it easier for them.

105

THE FINAL MOVE

Our burial is, in a certain sense, our final move. As a diplomat, I've moved many times in my life, and by now I'm thoroughly tired of it. But the worst moves have been cleaning out my father's, then my stepmother's, and finally my mother's homes. There were so many emotions mixed in.

Many older folks devote a great amount of time to sorting and cleaning things out while they're still alive. This is quite admirable, but very quickly becomes depressing. Thankfully there's no law that says you have to do any of this before you check out for good. I can only hope that my legacy will be reasonably large, to make it worthwhile for my kids to clean it all out in good humor.

106

THINKING OF TAKING ANYTHING WITH YOU TO YOUR GRAVE?

Most people want to have some personal items in their casket, just as the ancient Egyptians did. Things like letters and photographs, but also sweatpants and other things. I can understand people thinking that it must feel lonely down there in the ground, since death is comprehended in so many different ways. Perhaps we'll see each other again, perhaps not. Nobody knows.

This strengthens my belief that cremation is the best way to end your life on Earth. In cremation, most of the atoms which were once you and me will go up into the air like a pillar, to unite with other atoms under the blue sky. A bit is left behind to become fertilizer somewhere. I think these are comforting thoughts.

107

A FINAL GREETING

Others want to send a greeting from the other side, from the dead to the living. Our neighbor in Kivik, the author Fritiof Nilsson Piraten, definitely wanted to leave behind such a message. For that reason, he had these words carved on his tombstone at Ravlunda cemetery: "Here lie the ashes of a man who habitually put off everything until tomorrow. In the end, however, he bettered himself, and really did die the 31st of January, 1972."

A will is also a greeting, not to mention a direct order, from the dead. My advice is to let your heirs know roughly what it says while you're still alive. Otherwise, it may be a shock for some, and lead to disputes among your survivors.

Here's what the English poet Keats wanted on his headstone in Rome: "Here lies a man whose name was writ in water." The French author Stendahl chose this text, with which I identify very readily: "I loved, I wrote, I lived." The American author Kurt Vonnegut's suggestion isn't so bad, either: "Well, what did I say?" Now he's dead. I wonder if he got his way? You can't always trust your survivors.

As I so often think, our Danish neighbors seem to be a touch more clever than we Swedes, even when it comes to graves. This inscription is from a grave in Sjælland: "That was it." In any case, we can be envious of the dead for one reason: he is the consummate insider.

108

MANY WANT TO BE THERE FOR THEIR OWN FUNERALS

Occasionally, someone at a funeral reads a greeting from the deceased. If this is done correctly, it can be lovely. But it requires a lot from the dead person, so think carefully before trying it. As one of the dead, you should not be holding a debate. Besides, you have no way of defending your position.

Sometimes, the thoughts of one's own funeral can grow to unreasonable proportions. Many old folks consider who might come and who might "stand them up."

"I don't want to go to his funeral. Now he can't go to mine."

"I don't want to go to her funeral. She didn't go to mine."

I have heard both variations.

The older we get, the smaller the funeral will necessarily be. Perhaps there is some divine justice to the fact that he who dies younger gets the bigger funeral. At that time, one's life's work is unfinished, and the loss is actually greater. But that is all too rational a train of thought for those involved.

A better alternative is to arrange delightful birthday parties for your eightieth, eighty-fifth, ninetieth, and ninety-fifth birthdays. Write "grand finale" or "finissage" on the invitations and "no presents; just speeches."

That way, you'll get to hear all the fine speeches while you're still alive.

109

EVENTUALLY, WE ALL BECOME HISTORY

For every person who dies, a living memory of the past dies, too. Just like the tide on the beach, the memory recedes and is finally replaced some decades later by a historical account, written by people who experienced nothing of our lost world.

Eventually, we all become history, at the very least a number in a census.

Meanwhile, I continue stubbornly to plan my next book, my latest or my last—which one, I will never know. You might.

Life is full of opportunities. The best has yet to come.

So, good luck with the rest of life!